Crawlers

Poems by

Nathalie F. Anderson

The Ashland Poetry Press
Ashland University
Ashland, Ohio 44805

Acknowledgment is made to the following journals and anthologies in which these poems first appeared:

American Poetry Review (Philly Edition supplement*):* "The Miser"
Bonded Shores: "Tale"
Campbell Corner Poetry Prize web page (First Finalist in the competition for 2000; reprinted on the web page for the Journal of Mythic Arts, www.endicott-studio.com): "Shirt of Nettles, House of Thorns," "The Slaking"
Cumberland Poetry Review: "Floating Gardens," "Two Sorceries," "Mrs. Noah" (Robert Penn Warren Award 1997)
Louisville Review: "On Purchasing a Second Case of R. W. Knudsen Family Pomegranate Juice"
Madison Review: "My South" (Phyllis Smart Young Prize 1995)
Mad Poets Review: "Discipline"
New Millenium: "Baggage" (Second Place *New Millennium* Award for Poetry 1996)
Nimrod: "Formic Acid" (Honorable Mention Pablo Neruda prize competition 1997)
The Recorder: The Journal of the American Irish Historical Society: "Theseus Drops the Thread"
The Southern Anthology: "Spider Bite"
Southern Poetry Review: "Fort-Da"
/~xconnect (online edition): "Transpicuity"

"Sweat" was commissioned by Concerto Soloists of Philadelphia as the "summer" poem for their Philadelphia Four Seasons Project, first performed in 1996, a project in which Philadelphia poets, composers, and photographers collaborated in a multi-media concert based conceptually on Vivaldi's *Four Seasons*. I worked on this project with the composer Jonathan Holland and the photographer James Wasserman.

I am grateful to Swarthmore College and to the Pew Fellowships in the Arts for support in completing this manuscript; and to Abbe Blum, Betsy Bolton, Marcus Cafagña, Eileen Cahill, Syd Carpenter, Joy Charlton, Chin Woon-Ping, AV Christie, Lisa Coffman, Gigi and Buzz Crompton, Bob FitzSimons, Deborah Fleming, Daisy Fried, Eamon Grennan, Maggie Holley, Janet Kaplan, David Lloyd, Lee and Edith Potter, Elena Retfalvi, Peter Schmidt, Lisa Sewell, Cathy Staples, Kristina Straub, Margie Strosser, Tom Whitman, and Craig Williamson for comfort and advice.

Copyright © 2006 by Nathalie Anderson

All rights reserved. Except for brief quotations in critical reviews, this book, or parts thereof, must not be reproduced in any form without permission of the publisher. For further information, contact the Ashland Poetry Press, Ashland University, Ashland, OH 44805.

Printed in the United States of America

ISBN: 0-912592-59-1

Library of Congress Catalog Card Number: 2006924400

Cover: "Summer Evening with Inflictions" by Perky Edgerton
Used by permission of Rob and Val Hollister

Author photo: Elena Retfalvi

Ohio Arts Council
A STATE AGENCY
THAT SUPPORTS PUBLIC
PROGRAMS IN THE ARTS

*In memory of
Christopher "Kit" FitzSimons III
—my father—
who, before he died,
could still fling me a knowing look
from the grey innocence he was drowning in.*

Contents

I. Crawlers

Spider Bite/3
Crawlers/7
Distraction/10
Fort-Da/11
The Dream of the Dark/15

II. Sorceries

The Miser/19
Tale/20
Two Sorceries/21
Transpicuity/23
Shirt of Nettles, House of Thorns/25
Floating Gardens/28

III. Formic Acid

Formic Acid/33

IV. Baggage

Mrs. Noah/43
Baggage/46
My South/51
Footwork/54
Theseus Drops the Thread/58
Two Little Songs About Love/59
Sweat/60
Girls at the Hemingford Grey Regatta/61
Out/62

V. The Slaking

Two Last Things/67
Black Hole/70
On Purchasing a Second Case of R. W. Knudsen Family
    Pomegranate Juice/78
The Slaking/80

Notes/83

"Lies will flow from my lips..."
—Virginia Woolf
A Room of One's Own

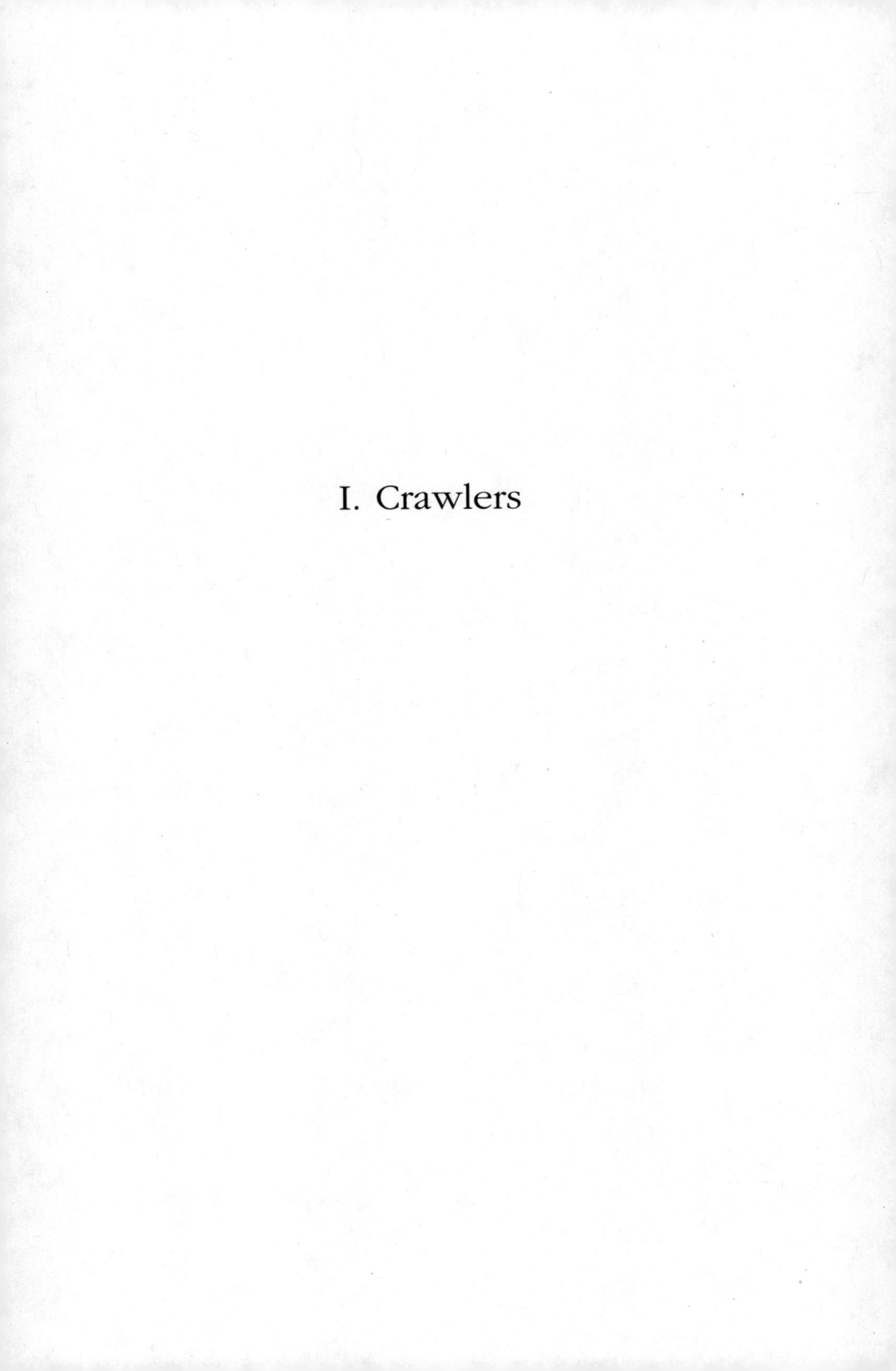

I. Crawlers

Spider Bite
in memory of Robert Heyward Mercer

1. The Pretty

A bead of jet set in a wisp of lace—
what child would choose a play-toy so

Victorian? Even then, the eye for
exquisite detail—the fleck of red

visible only when turned just so,
the tiny rakish crimson bow-tie

taut with implication. Imagine
the gasp when he brought it in—death

in the dining room, dangled striking distance
from a chubby fist, a puckish mouth,

an eye—the last bright bead of a
mourning brooch hung by a fraying thread, and

every heart going pitapat. Pretty
boy, Fauntleroy—pity! pity! He was

born like that—always hurrying
to share the beauty he found with

those least likely to appreciate it.

2. Negative

Something mean about the way she'd pose us
straight into the light, eyes going pink

as a rabbit's, the blue leaching out
in puny tears, hands flung up against

the sting. Stand straight! Head up! Don't squint! Smile!
To anyone listening it might have seemed

the exasperation of love. Three of us
in our Easter best—the step-children,

the adopted boy. I can still hear
the hard-bitten pride: "Nobody ever

raised a hand to those children, nobody
even sent them to the yard for a switch

except they asked for it." And here we are,
egg-baskets raised like talismans, the fake grass

gossamer around us, not a bruise
visible, asking for it, shoved face-first

into the fist of the withering sun.

3. The Rigging

First a cable to bridge the masts, twisted
boom-thick, stout enough to hold a body

steady in a gale. Then a line dropped to
anchor the triangulating shrouds, and

last the stays, clew lines, halyards spiraling
out from the silken hub. Any sailor

would do, but where did he find so many,
my cousin, in our land-locked town? Imagine

the web subtle enough to catch a vibration
and return it, keen enough to snare

the gleam in an eye and refract it back.
The crew sang with exhilaration, though

beyond their life-lines swollen predators
widened their eyes, clicked their self-righteous jaws.

Robbie, listen. Every dawn the rope-men
rewind their sturdy spirals, devouring

the sticky silk, retracting every sign.

4. Positive

See here? Photos of the Widow, nothing
on the Recluse. No blame—nobody knew,

before the fifties, the harm it could do. Bitten,
the flesh of his leg boiled up against the skin,

scalding it iridescent, glossy as
any keloid, before it began to

eat itself away. Look—the carapace
fiddles its optical illusion: first

the pegs, and then—ah—scrolled, bellied, waisted,
the violin. Days later, I found one

evasive and inscrutable among
the papers on my desk. I looked and looked

before I struck him down. Where was it, Rob?
Fugitive in the tool shed? Closeted

with the winter coats? Inconspicuous
in the sock drawer? Shadowy guest on the

wrong side of the bed? Here between the lines?

5. The Moult

I remember like it was yesterday:
three children sent to an empty room, and

I mean empty—not a piece of paper,
not a chair, the rough-dyed carpet so raw

it scorched us through our shorts—left to ourselves
to play. So obvious, yet imagine

the shock of saying the words out loud: "Not
happy," the youngest of us open-mouthed,

open-eyed, as if the world at last made
sense. Let me be clear: no one saw it as

cruelty, us least of all—step-children,
adopted boy, at home in the only

world we knew, bad attitudes all and glad
of the privacy, little spiders

seething in venom, daring the bite,
digesting our true selves, peeling away from

the old skin, claiming the pain as our own.

Crawlers

The whine. The whack. Blood on the wall. She was
smiting the fatted mosquits again. How
the days thickened: the first shimmer of gnats—
a skein fugitive and incandescent as
the ghost of her dead mother, keening
pianissimo, with an underbreath
of miasma—that fine haze sweltering
by noon to a spattering scud, fruit flies
clotted over what fruit there was, dinky
but determined; and, in the spent breath of
sultry afternoon, the thunk and bristle
of house flies, careening, gadding, thronging—
hoarse hoboes, tasting the world through their feet.

The house lurching on scrawny legs, the yard
swept bare, the torn screen tacked to a warped frame,
the air sticky with peaches: she knew not
to trust whatever lived there, and for sure
the place was ripe with flies—each smear of peach
raspy with them; each sodden paper bag,
snaking with peels of the furred skin, grumbly
with their shambling; each sugared jar and bowl
thicketed. She could feel them in her throat
each time she swallowed. "Doesn't the princess
like peaches then?" Through cracks in the floor, when
she hung her head, she saw them at home there,
scuffing the dirt with their rustling wings. And

at dusk, boiling out of puddled water
into the dank air, the mosquitoes came
dancing, anorectic ballerinas
with their mince, their traipse, their sashay, their flounce,
their limping flights, their gallivants, peevish
and sneering, somebody's fey god-mothers but
surely not hers—fingers spindled again
and again, bled till she blistered, the skin

peeling up riddled from the bloated flesh,
thin as a whisper, as a forgotten
promise. What she could count on: ants hanging
by their jaws; skirling horseflies; swaggering
wasps; a hail of bees. By herself, at night,

as the tub filled, naked as she was born,
she mapped the archipelagoes of bites,
measly volcanoes rising open-mouthed
and lurid from her petal skin, ringing
her waist, her groin, ankles at the sock-line—
wherever the elastic nipped and the
chiggers burrowed. Nail polish choked them out
but what did she want with polish, a girl
of her age? Struck by hot water, how they
flared, sizzled, seared, though the red speck nestling
in the pit of the fumarole suckled
serenely on. Gnats like pepper in the nose,
fruit flies coughed from the back of the tongue, flies

bruising an eye, rough and tumble under
the lid—how she learned privacy, her thoughts
guarded all day against her chaperones,
her urgent companions, until, alone
with the crawling dark—gnats silent, fruit flies
fallen, the curtains beaded heavy with
sleeping flies—dark scuttled over her, false
lashes whisking her cheek; brushed at her mouth,
furring her lips, leaving the bitter bloom
behind. Cold and eerie at the window,
fire-flies shed their ghost-green light; chalk shrill,
hysteric, crickets scraped leg over wing;
mosquito hawks swung scimitar shadows.

In stories, no motherless girl is left
without solace. Doves coo her home; horses
press velvet muzzles into her palm; goats
offer cheese; cats purr wisdom; even ants
carry their weight. In the skittery kitchen

long after midnight, she flicked the light switch
on, off, on, to watch the roaches scatter,
shitting eggs as they ran—the seed roach, black
and tan; the small soft auburn German; thick
rusty Americans; the clattering
Palmetto: not one eye meeting hers, not
one slick mandible parting to pass a
message on. Of course, she only tells you

half of it: never how the lady-bug
flew home with such purpose; how the daddy-
long-legs sidled along the base-board, shared
her corner; how the roly-poly rolled
up, infant armadillo, at the mere
whisk of a pine straw; how butterflies kissed;
how leaf hoppers strayed through meadowed hair to
ride a mossy neck; how fire-flies lit
paper lanterns, spangled the dark yards; how
crickets counted her to cadenced sleep; how
dawn curtained her windows with green lace wings.
A thousand blameless lives—forthright, homely,
decent, unassuming—but every day

she ate the weevil with the flour, she
smothered the earwig on the pillow, she
broke the flea between her bloody thumbs, she
wrenched the tick away and burned him, she
clawed the devils from her flesh. Heart racing,
skin cold, eyes sharp, mouth dry, throat clamping shut
from the yellow-jacket's barb: nice girls don't
scratch, however much it itches. Cradled
in silence, absence, memory, folded
in the deepest womb of dream, how she reached
for that dark and lustrous blossom, to pluck
a stem of beetles, crawling the shape of
petals they had eaten, the perfect rose.

Distraction

For days the thunderflies were thick
on her skin, *broderie vivante,*
broderie anglaise. No one else
seemed troubled, no other thumb rubbed
ceaseless over neck and shoulder,
cheek and chin. Was she the blackwork
princess, then, stitched heel to head with silk
no other soul could feel? Something
was bound to break—arm, heart, window,
the sky's white china, flat and dull—
why not this stitchery? She'd like
to fray it off, rip the seams, peel
back the pale skin, tack its edges,
work a clean overcast, open
her heart. Who needs lightning slashing
when you're worn so thin, a single
seed stitch might break through? Dangling threads
went on crawling the circuits of
her ears, snaking among the hairs
of her head, stirring the hollows
in back of her knees. Who could think
of being open-hearted with
this fine net ever drawing tight
its lithe patchwork, its black lace veil?

Fort-Da

1. Flare

First it was dark and then it was light. That's
how it must have been. Under my head
his leg must have shifted from gas to brake
to gas. Look at that, he must have said.

Under my head—braids fraying, bangs whisked up damp
at the cowlick, cheek creased with the crush
and crumple of his summer-weight grey slacks—
under my head his leg shifted. That's how

it must have been. I can just about taste
the milk-and-water consolation of
my suckled thumb, just about make out
the desolation he wore then, his face

lit by the passing head-lamps, the slight jog
in the bridge of his nose, the slight rift in his chin.
Look at that, he said—a barn burning! Light
and then dark. I stared where he pointed,

into the night, and never saw what he
said he saw—the brave braided girl, running
for water, bringing hope in a bucket,
quieting the animals, saving the day.

2. Fog

First it was clear and then it was cloud, and
by morning the world had gone. The light
rose slow and pearly. Condensation wept
down the inside of the pane. When he braced

the casement open, the air itself was thick,
thick and brisk, and the little hairs curled back
from around my eyes. Whatever had stood
across the street—apartment block, gas pump

with its flying horse, the traffic lights faithful
up Main Street—all blotted out; just like that
we were on our own, grey air guarding the corner
and beyond it the empty white. That's

how it was, how it was going to be. He
swung his arm like he was planning to dive
or fly. Look at that, he said. He wasn't
looking at me. I can just about smell

that strange chilled air, feel the concrete gritty
under a knee, slick to a palm, the vault
off the shoulder like wiping your hands as
you make the jump, crouch down for a turn: leap-frog.

I looked where he pointed, never saw
those curly-haired boys
flinging themselves through mist, trusting that the street
they couldn't see went on before them.

3. Blink

Somewhere on the field the ball comes down. Would you
look at that? he says, the exasperated fan
on the bench beside me, and I'm as smoothly
sympathetic as the deeply ignorant can be.

If it had been a snake it would have bit me.
And what if it had? What then? Now you see it
and now you don't, the dog's third snarl, the ferryman's
blind eye, the glance that erases the love

it looks for. Practice makes perfect—I've grown
sharp-eyed, can count by the thousands now
the lovely, miraculous, fleeting things
I haven't seen: the kingfisher's burnt belly

and azure wing; the fox caught in the head-lights,
fore-leg extended; the significant look
at the dinner table; the eagle's circling,
the falcon's plunge; the opening yawn

of the night-blooming cereus; shoes hanging
from a wire; the tadpole losing its tail;
intelligence rising suddenly into
a child's eye. You point, I look straight there

but wherever I look I'm not seeing
the one thing worth watching for; whatever
I'm looking at, it's absence, absence,
the one aching absence that still fills my eye.

4. Choke

Straight lanes oozing tar from Orangeburg
to Elloree, tires ripping it up
like a bandaid from skin—it's my Daddy
in his Chevy, the hot breath of the South

roaring in and past him, slapping his face
and slicking his glasses, curling the black hairs
from his wrist up his arm. He's rolled his cuffs
to just below the elbow; he's loosened his tie

with its smart knot and its bold white lines;
one hand tapping to the radio's thick static;
one hand open, cupping the air; the easy
inattention, the scrub-pine blurring, when

WHAP! a whip at the eye, the wheel swerving,
and he's sleeved in gore, a bird's head like a child's fist
hung through the bat-wing, the neck's hinge snapped, car
filling with feathers as the heavy body

beats and beats itself in at the window and
against the door. The lurch, the stench, the hot blood
flecking the rear-view, spots before his eyes.
Of all the pheasant's handsome feathers—

the cocked crown, the barred cinnamon, the deep
forest green—he brought back not one, nor any
bite of the meat. He came home shaking
in a borrowed suit, a dent in the car door

though inside it was clean where they'd hosed it.
He'd pull out the choke with the door still hanging open,
sit there uneasy before he cranked the car.
Smell that blood? he'd say, but I never did,

never saw anything like that on his hands.

The Dream of the Dark

You have a friend who has forgotten you,
who has forgotten his own name. When he
comes to stay he makes himself small, he
clenches his teeth, sits on his hands so they
won't tell, screws shut his eyes so you won't see,

whoever you are. Here is a word and
here is a thing. He holds one in one hand,
one in the other—he has forgotten
what comes next. He might clap his hands, he might
fold them together, he might open them

and let the birds fly back to their
branch, the sands sift back to the shore. You think
he could catch them, and he could, he could, but
is it worth the work, worth closing his hand?
He feeds the parakeet, he pets the cat,

but what names can he call them by? He lives
in a tower with a long stair, steps that
spiral down and down. At the bottom is
a well, and every night he draws from it
what he can. You can visit him there, and

he'll call you by name, the secret name you've
long forgotten. He'll call a spade a spade
and dig with it, dig halfway to China
for the boy he was. Whatever lives there
rises, wrinkles the well water, breathes deep,

subsides. Is it worth the work? Sand castles
melt back into the sea. This all belongs
to you now. Dig deep. Grip hard. Drink your fill.
He has nothing more to give you, stranger.
The stair gets longer. The well runs dry.

II. Sorceries

The Miser

First night together, and he said "Don't—
don't ever, don't you ever write about
me." First thing from his mouth, and it took
her breath: he saw how she was capable,
saw what words—her words—might do.

Scraped his nails down the pale silk skin
of her fore-arm. "Don't write about this," he said
and bent her little finger back. She felt
like she'd swallowed gold: all that sick wealth
inside her that she'd never get to spend.

Tale

The goat boys with their yellow eyes
hang out on the corner where three streams meet.
Do you want to play? They nudge each other.
They can make you if they like.

Only the angels have such fair hair,
or so Gran said before she knew.
Good morning! Good morning! They
won't open their hard mouths.

Who can say what they might want
until they want it? They share
a yellow look, shake their butt heads.
They'll want something any minute now.

Thought you'd edge past? Nothing gets by them,
clattering after, white beards flying.
You can be girl with her fat basket.
You can be troll under her dark bridge.

White brows, white beards—is it only the angels
never utter a sound, never have to?
They rear on their hind legs, taller than men now.
They eat the branches. They eat the trees.

Two Sorceries

I. Altered Sky

The blade was sharp and the fever was high.
Somewhere a quarrel sprang into air.
Surgeons, their backs turned, circling the body.
Blood in the throat. The neck skinned back.

Somewhere a quarrel sprang into air.
The needle was hot and the thread was long.
Blood in the throat. The neck skinned back.
Snick snack sang the blade that clipped each stitch.

The needle was hot and the groove was scratched,
Frayed thread of a sound unwound in an ear.
Snick snack sang the blade that cut her loose.
Her fingers closed on a foreign hand.

A threat unwound in an open ear.
The throat was slit and the neck was wrung.
Her fingers closed, a foreign hand.
The vein was dry and the mouth was parched.

The throat was slit and the neck was wrung;
The tongue was bitter, the tongue was sharp;
The vein was dry and the mouth was parched.
Remember nothing. Remember it all.

The tongue was bitter, the tongue was sharp;
The sun rose white in an altered sky.
Remember nothing. Remember it all.
The fall of petals in a silent room.

The sun rose white and bloomed in air.
The blood was bright and the fever high.
The fall of petals in a silent room.
Surgeons, their backs turned, circling the body.

II. Spirit Emporium

First thing out of hospital she sat down
with the catalogs she'd hoarded since the spring
and everything she wanted she clipped out.

Meticulous, she scissored every prize
free of its dross—each push-up bra, limpid
as a skin of oil on water, she sliced

clear of its flesh, its raised and yearning arms,
the parings spiraling from her steely
hand, crumpling themselves in origami

eccentricities, a hodge-podge settling
to a flimsy patchwork, a gift-wrapped bed.
Under the pillow, she banked plenitude:

paper furnishings for paper houses,
paper clothes for paper dolls—red velvet
blotting paper: a Russian collared blouse;

transparent mauve rice-paper: wine goblets,
their swirl of pin-prick bubbles a paper
promise of champagne. Wreathed pomegranates,

artichokes. A desk with secret drawers where
letters could be safely lost. The lilac
iridescence of glistered Roman glass—

earrings of peeled skin, choker of silver
bruises.
      Later, she would strike match after
match, and spirit each treasure into air,

stocking the icy empty smoky shelves of
that vast emporium where pestilence
might shop to its heart's content, might buy up

all her burning desires, and leave her be.

Transpicuity

So, my good window of lattice, fare thee well;
Thy casement I need not open, for I look through thee.
—*All's Well That Ends Well*

She looked me through, one way
to clear the air. Dust
settled itself, clouds
sucked themselves dry, the very sun
ran through me: clear-eyed
and empty-hearted, I could see
how still I shadowed her.

The dragonflies were
keener, scouring holes
in the air, gusty windows
to sail their sticks through—
black and blue, shiny
with effort, riding the rapids
of shivering glass.

Or the spiders, guying blade to blade,
cordoning the lawn: reef knot,
sheep shank, cat's paw. "We'll
overlook it," she said, "this time"—
precisely the instant they
snared the sun, and the meadow vanished
in that fiery mantilla.

She gave me a ring, a little window on the flesh,
framed in verdegris or verditer, latticed
with gold, and when I slipped it on, the skin beneath
gleamed bright as pomegranate, blazed with rubies, rich life
pulsing at the wicket. Off, it was dull,
the finger safe, the casement clear. I saw myself
as she sees me, jeweled in blood, my own blood.

There's a lattice lashes make as dark comes down
and night after night she waits there. "We'll
see it through," she promises, transparent
as words can make her. Oh, I see through it—
the spine of the lie, infinitely articulate;
the sputtering gut; the two-tongued heart—
cave fish, phosphorescent; white clouds in a black sky.

Shirt of Nettles, House of Thorns
in awed esteem for Alice Maher, who made these things

1. Strange Seed

You plant the strange seed to see how it grows—
a beanstalk to the clouds, a better tomato,
poison apple, deadly nightshade, kudzu—
always a surprise. So the little ruddy rose hip

yawns into a peony; the grain of salt
takes fire, puffs out its cheeks of glass; the seed pearl
complicates in porcelain crinolines;
splinters thicken to hard block; the dust bunny

kicked and wincing, forgotten under the bed,
rowls itself into the junk-yard dog—that's it
in a nutshell: each snail distilling
the cowl on its back, the husk it was born to.

2. House of Thorns

A nest for Thumbelina nestled into moss,
pied-à-terre among the *pommes-de-terre*,
basking and burnished as a cinnamon cat
licked into spits and glossy with tending.

Look again: it's the bristling boll of sweet-gum or
sycamore or buck-eye—some spurred species—squared
to a folk profile: peaked roof, high gable
spiky with thorn—a closed house, impervious,

leathering into prickly isolation.
Where's the girl ripe for piercing, who shuttered
her windows and latched fast her doors? Where's the chink
to press an eye to? Where's the coy lip to kiss?

Oh prince, rip your hands, rip your heart out. Someone
walked through the briars with her eyes wide open,
laying her hand deliberately against each thorn—
thick at the base, fanged at the tip, each cat-claw

picked for its precision, slicing the thumb
to the bone. Someone dried them, aligned them,
mortared them straight. Someone knew you'd come looking.
She built that house, made that bed, walked away.

3. Shirt of Nettles

Thick in the thicket gooseberries hung their lanterns
from two-inch spines; raspberries ripened into jam
on razor-edged canes. She held the gloves out
so disparagingly, you saw you couldn't win.

Ringed round by briars muscled thick as snakes,
there's not much scope for turning. Bees laced themselves
through the fretwork. The smug smile: "It's only nettles."
          Your hands
puffed white with the sting. Blackbirds in the hawthorn,

beaks open for the bite. Between morning
and evening a quick snap of the tongue: fling out
the changeling cursed with a quickness
too sharp for her own good. Imagine going wittingly

to pluck the nettle, leaves caught in an apron
and every slightest brush a skin-popping shock. Greening,
flattening, pinning, stitching—bite your pillow,
claw at the air, skin welting along the spine and rib

of each fine seam, each particular leaf. How long
before you strip it off, bled light as a feather—
a pain you made to grow out of,
something for Good Will, last year's fashion.

4. Ever After

Once upon a time—as long ago as that
and all forgiven. The curb falls from the tongue;
eyes cry themselves to clarity; the girl
wakes up, runs to the window, brushes

her glowing hair. But close your eyes and
it's the flay tongue, it's the whip hand, it's
the acid bath, the scald eye, the happy
ever after: fanged house, shirt of flame.

Floating Gardens

1.

When they came to the island, they became
the people of the island, they became
the people of the lake. The land was lean
and the people were meager, but the lake
was deep with fish: their crush and fidget
rattled the reeds and churned the lily roots;
their jostle and flirt startled the water
into overlapping o's; when they slid
between the lily pads, they made the depths
shiver, like something swimming through a grave.

When they came for the fish, the reeds rattled
and the fish rippled away. But they were
the people of the lake: they cut the reeds,
they cut paths through the reeds, they cast the reeds
over the lilies until the lilies
sank with the weight. As they whisked the quick fish
free of the water, flailing like a heart
that gasps for its lost home, they became the
people of the blade. They cut the channels
deep, they banked the silt. The reeds and lilies

rotted away. But when the green arrows
of willow struck root there, they saw what they
must become: they saw the circles of jade,
they saw the temples step from the water
into the sun, they saw the mountain rise
like a lily and thrust out its petaled
heart, they saw the mist of flowers, they saw
the gods rain down. Blood snakes through water and
earth quakes, but the splitting seed will anchor you:
stand steady, floating on your flowering heart.

2.

When the step-child was alone, a white bird
sang to her from the willow. If you can
braid your hair, it sang, you can braid these boughs;
and she did: she cut the tender withies,
whippy and green, and she braided them thick
as her thumb. The bird twittered. If you can
twist a rope, it sang, you can weave a cup;
and she did: she crossed the braids of willow
and wove the supple withies round and round,
the web tight, the wattle strong. If you can

dig a grave, the bird sang next, you can
fill a net. Well, she did that too. She stole
heart in mouth to her mother's grave, she wept
hand to heart to soften the earth, she dug
fist over hand, and the basket was filled.
If you can cry a river, it sang now,
you can launch a boat.
      You know how it ends,
don't you? How it rode low in the water,
tipsy and precarious; how it sailed
to a far country; how it rooted there;

you know what fruit grew on that tree; you know
who plucked that fruit; you know the palaces,
the singing birds. But here is something you
may not know: in spite of everything the
bird taught her—celestial navigation,
propagation, duty, riddling, basketry—
she never believed she would get away,
never believed she would root herself or
fling her branching heart in air, though this
outlandish story nearly always comes true.

III. Formic Acid

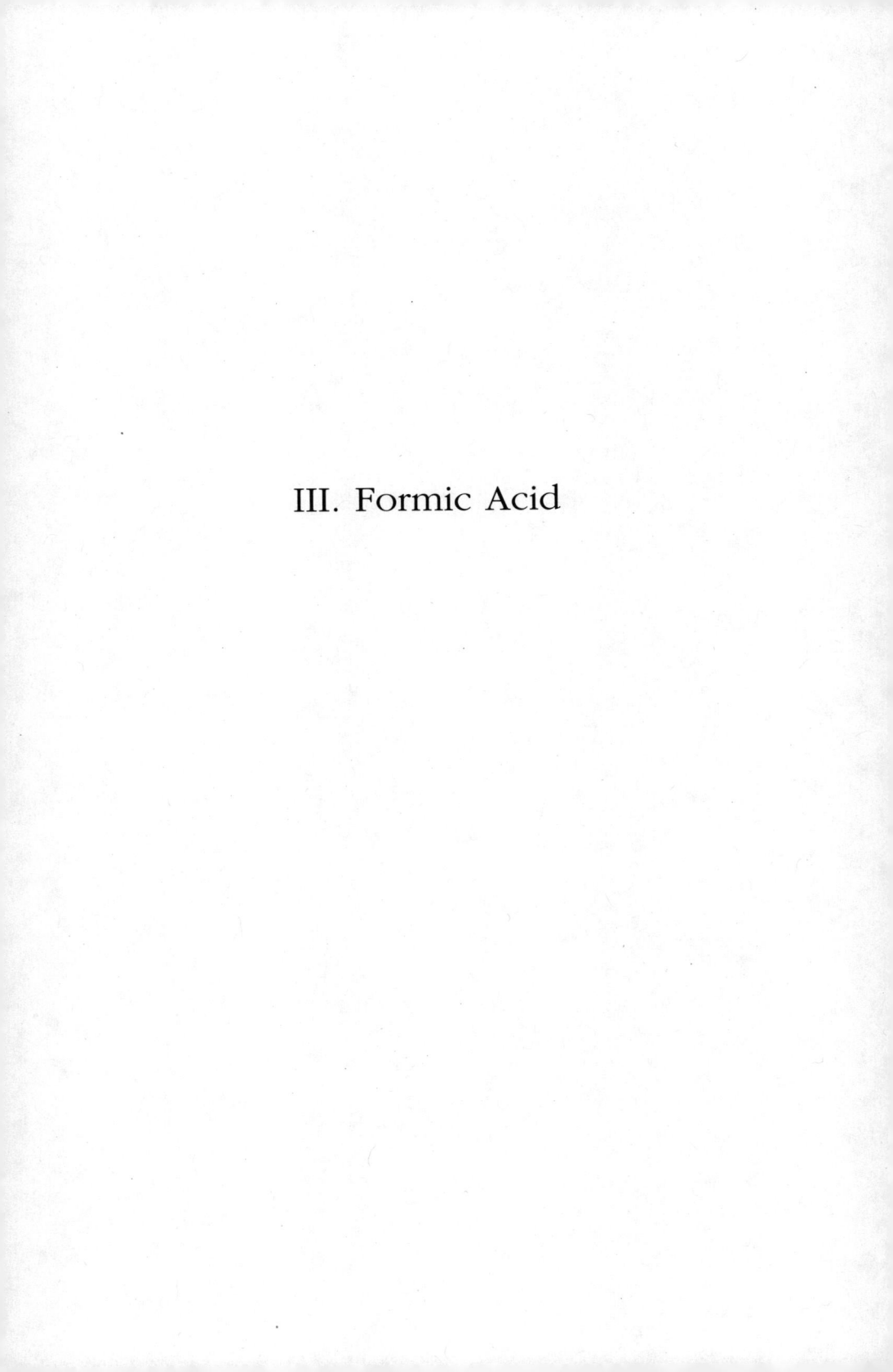

Formic Acid
in memory of Nathalie Heyward FitzSimons and with respect
for Albert Schweitzer, whose photograph so intrigued her

I.

All there in black and white, and we were
open-mouthed, my gran and me—what that man
would stand for! She'd knock her knuckle on
the photograph, cock her eye, and we'd
whoop and whoop at his daft gallantry—
the giant waiting for the ants to pass, that
icon of eccentricity. Held back
forever by the camera's flash,
the shin-bone shining through thin flesh, tendons
roped and knotted at the ankle, gnarled feet
striking in their tacky sandals, each sinew
taut with forbearance: choosing to do
no harm, choosing to watch his step, his
every step. There in black and white, and we

believed it. Now, I don't know—that cheap book,
its too-slick paper, its motile ink
clinging to the hand like margarine
half-liquid in the heat, unctuous
with a hint of grit; the captioned words
scattering at a touch, trailing their
smeared and broken letters; the image
greying so quickly beyond the clear-cut
resolution of foot and calf and thigh;
the ants themselves concealed among
the shifting values of the page. "Wouldn't
hurt a fly," she'd say, squinting her eyes
for a better look, and we'd hoot and
holler, while I thought of the tse-tse,

the sleep no one could wake from, the mule
distended in the drainage ditch, maggots
in the eye. Where did he draw the line,
and him a doctor? Believe it or not,
the tribes use soldier ants to stitch their wounds—
goaded to bite across a cut and then
beheaded. And driver ants, believe
or not, will dismantle the very
mantis devouring them. Each spring she'd
hunker in the yard to split the iris,
the muscles in her speckled legs ropy
with crouching. "Live and let live," she'd say,
savoring absurdity, while the ants
passed by oblivious on every side.

II.

Black on white: a dotted line short-cutting
a corner off the kitchen linoleum,
lickety-split from door-jamb to pantry—
ants on the prowl. And in the next room
hunched in his red chair, keeping silent
account, the man who wouldn't stand for it.
We had to love him, my brother and me,
the motherless chicks he'd taken in and
raised by hand—not that it was his hand
that did the raising. "Tell me this," he'd say,
knocking his knuckle on the air, as if
against some whippersnapper's chest: "How
could a grown woman think or say or do
such and such a thing?" A grown woman:

in the white kitchen, methodical, she'd
mix herself a coffee float—black coffee,
white ice cream, the rich *café au lait*. She'd
drink it down and then, methodical, she'd
scour the glass, the sink, the counter
spick and span, while in the next room he'd

be calculating: "Did she tell you
about those ants in the pantry?" as if
it were a joke they shared between them. Words,
dogmas, propositions: trails laid down
for us to swallow, the dotted line
held out for us to sign, cutting edge,
double cross, sell out, intoxicating
scent of sophistry. Believe it or not,

the ants of India whip each other,
antennae lashing out in rituals
of dominance. Believe it or not,
the slash of the trap-jaw ant back-flips it
bodily through the air. We watched our
every step, unwilling Myrmidons,
hoping to side-step the traps he'd set
for us to trigger. "Live and let live,"
I tried once, but he was scathing: "There's
black and white, night and day, proper and
not. And you so smart: explicate that." It's
where I learned to look behind the clear-cut,
where I learned that the silence of resistance can
flip in air, twisted into tacit consent.

III.

So many children they ran out of names,
called the youngest—a girl—after the
oldest boy: Nathaniel, Nathalie. That's
how she accounted for the odd-ball h
silent at her very center. Not till
years later, watching the credits scroll
white on black in a French cinema,
did I realize there might be other
explanations. Oldest boy, youngest girl—
it bound them, their name, inextricably:
when lightning slashed him, it struck her too

in the dark house four fields away, as if
the sky had knocked its knuckle on her chest,
ozone raising her every hair, stinging
the goose flesh. It had me open-mouthed,
that story, but she told my brother
something else entirely. Maybe
the past is always grey like this, threaded
thick with false connection; the shocking flash—
the white on black—necessarily
fictive. I have two photographs of her
before I knew her. In one, a child
cuts laughing eyes at the camera, cute,
acute, like the woman she'll grow into;
in the next, plump as a peasant, round cheeks
and shadowed eyes, she's someone else entirely,
while her thin husband, arms crossed and breath held
in a tight sum, is all sharp angles

even then. Believe it or not, herder ants
hang grappled together in living bowls
cradling their queen, their young, their flocks and herds,
domesticated mealy-bugs. Believe it
or not, the only known colony of
Leptanillines—each pin-prick sister
stitched into the glistening tissue
rippling white on black through the tree's rotted heart—
that incandescence seeped away entirely
before the witness knew what he'd seen.
In this last photo, four generations,
four Nathalies: Nannie, Bid, Nat, Lally—
not one of us called by our given name.
Neighbors called her Fitzie. Nathaniel was long gone.

IV.

How many years went by after she last said,
and so clear no one could misconstrue it,
"I want to die"? Twelve at least—stroke after
stroke towards midnight, the heavy knuckle
at the door, the mouth gaping. The last time
I saw her, they'd tied a soft pink bow
at her throat, they'd pinned a camellia
at her breast, they'd permed her hair, tucked in
her teeth, perched her glasses on her nose,
strapped her upright in her chair, shut in
with the unspeakable. As the hours
tip-toed past, what was there for her to hear
but white mist rising, or black night falling? What
to breathe but white air, or black air? "Shut your trap,"

he used to say, "before the flies light
on your tongue." The last time I saw her,
her three-year-old great-grand-son fed her
raisins from a box, fat and wrinkled
as flies, her mouth as wide, as ravenous,
as undiscriminating as a
nestling's. Nothing to be done: no plug
to pull; and though I squirmed in my chair
sitting through the sanctimonious cant—
the shining Christ-like sanctity of
that emptied life—there's nothing I knew
different to do, while her strong heart
sidled serenely, treacherously on.
Believe it or not, a fallen ant

will lie unnoticed in the nest for days
until the stench of decay renders it
perceptible. Believe it or not,
worker-slaves captured by Amazon ants
tend and defend the captors' young as though
true sisters of the queen, disarmed by scent,
their own entangled with the reek of the

burnished slavers. So used to stepping
aside, she twisted her hip the day
they buried him, trying to walk straight
across the kitchen floor. Imagining
my own stark future, I hope against all hope
she passed those twelve years dreaming the thick
familiar honeyed odor, the home nest, the tribe.

V.

It'll happen again any day now:
crocus give way to daffodil and then
to tulip; the earth recover its
precarious balance and turn its face
to the sun; and in my cold dark basement
the ants will rise, quickening out of the
solid floor, seething up through scratched cement
like steam through a sieve, swarming, flying blind.
The white light of the laundry room draws them
in Egyptian plagues, into the surging
washer, through the dryer's filter into
desiccating air, up the light cord's
dangling ladder to eternity,
unlikely angels. I don't stand for it:

I strike them from my hair and eyes; I
smite them trembling from the shivering air; I
walk all over them, snapping the struts
of flimsy paper wings, cracking their
chitinous backs till my foot-soles slicken.
The night she died, my brother called me,
sobbing: nothing to be anymore
except grown up, no place to put a foot
other than on the earth that holds her.
He's looking for solidity, for
the sharp definition, the clarity
of black and white. The ground I walk on
is riddled, rifted, threaded, seamed, veined;
its particles—black, white, red, brown—jumbled

by the steady traffic; each grain of that
debris abraded daily, scraped, scuffed, scoured
towards imperceptibility. Believe
or not, the ants below a town
out-weigh the women, men, and children
walking its streets. Believe or not,
the heat of daily life quickening in
an ant hill will melt away a winter's
blanket of snow. As dawn rises, I watch
the basement door gradually brighten,
light knocking my knuckles, stinging muscles
twisted, whipped by the strain. Tell me: this year
will I let them fight their own battles,
follow their own queen, fend for themselves?

IV. Baggage

Mrs. Noah
(Toy Ark)

I. Bulk

Two deck-hands to trundle her off-ship,
I'll bet, and two doors wheezed back to grease her
into the grocery. Thighs water-logged and
belly rolling, she's ballasted deep
as a Spanish galleon, scudding
the sea-lanes from dairy to freezer, from
bread to juice, from soup to nuts, broad-beamed and
swag-bellied, her sea-legs bloated blubbery.

Every woman there sucks in her gut. It's
hell to lose, that spread below the waist, that
flesh luxuriant, however much you
try to starve it out, try to run it lean,
try pissing it away. Each time I try,
my face goes haggard, my breast dries up, though
the jeans still pucker, still refuse the zip.
What I am: a peg set on a barrel.

If she walked the plank, don't imagine she
would shrink, don't imagine she'd slip her flesh
like fingers from a glove. No, her bulk would
buoy her, skirts bellying and slumping,
a slack parasol, a wraith jellyfish
trailing its strings through all the flooded seas,
walking the cold waters, thin arms out-stretched,
raven for the left hand, dove for the right.

II. Offering

My Gami came to me thin as tissue paper
wrapped tight over a gift, the wonder of it
shining through. Her neat head was bound with braids
of silver, and once at night I saw it loose
and rippling, a fall of water reaching
to her knees. Print shirt-waist tidy even
in the garden, where she cultivated
ferny fairy roses, their scrolled buds unfurling

to a bloom no wider than a dime: fragrance
settling its little cloak about me; moss
raising its tiny antlers; and flying unearthly
above us, the jet-black squirrel, the pearl-white jay.
While my Nannie wrestled water-color paper
onto the paste-board, bracing it flat
where it buckled, sinking the tack with a thumb
black and stippled from the yard: azalea,

  camellia—the showy short-lived blooms; strong stock,
steady root. Luckies rustling the pocket of her
seersucker shorts; sun lighting the white flame
of her hair; butterscotch spilling into the sink:
a humdinger of a day. The slender,
the sturdy; the earth, the air: yes, when I
opened the Ark they stood there two by two,
each offering me half of everything she had.

III. Wake

If you're quick you can trace the trail we leave
even in high seas, the surface soapy
for a good ten minutes afterwards, then
slickening to a bolt of fine satin
unfolding and re-folding behind us.
And the prow doesn't knife through: it rises,
falls—shears opening and closing, flinging
lace sleeves to either side. Nothing so white—

milk with no touch of cream in it, melting
back into the blue-black waves. Below deck,
it's true, every nuance of a swell beats
and batters you against the cabin walls,
rattles you down the passageways, churns you
buttery, but here on deck we assume
the sea's horizon, ride out all weathers. I
know what we look like, our barn of a boat,

a wood block marking the nursery carpet,
my thick bell of a skirt, arms painted skinny
across my thin chest. But look: the sweep of it,
shot silk, slub silk, a cloak flung back, velvet
edged with ermine, dusted with pearl. I hold it
in my hand: nothing so evanescent,
nothing so weighty as this watered globe.
I'm where I'm pegged for. No gale blows me down.

Baggage

I.

Every arm in town had its hand out
towards her. That's what she saw: a street of hands.
And no tableau of poignant supplication,
no sinuous flowering of cupped palms—
no: she walked a gauntlet of gesticulation,
hands busy picking, pinching, plucking the air:
shop girls clutching the breeze beside her sleeve;
transport boys stroking the heat off an engine
or throttling, for her, a fictive steering wheel
down fictive switch-back hills; jewelers
tugging the fictive silver at her ears;
hawkers scooping fictive rice into her
dumb-struck open jaws. The heat was on her,
sweating her rancid. This wasn't what she came for.

At each canonical hour, cock-light
to cock-shut, she tried to scour the gold dust
from her feet and hands. She'd never noticed it
at home; this wasn't who she was, this mother lode,
this golden calf, this fortune on the hoof—
though who else was she: leisured, well-heeled,
      far from home?
Morning, noon, and night, passed like a thinning coin
      from hand
to hand, she came to know the texture of each touch,
thick irony in the calloused thumb, bent wit
in the crooking finger. Not one, she learned,
was open for a hand-out: not temple children
offering for sale their single perfect blooms;
not beach girls roping her with bangles
strung with soda straw and seed: an empty hand

demands; the hands she emptied hazarded
refilling in return. Beyond the fingers
to the wrist, up the pushed-back sleeve, along
the aching shoulder, higher, higher, to the eye—
each appraised, appraising, each with its own
agenda, its secret lust, its secret
generosity, its own sufficient
compromise. So, when the market woman
with kilos left to sell split with a stained thumb-nail
the wrinkled shell of the passion fruit, steadied
the slithery seeds with the heel of her unwashed palm,
and held the dusty little cup up to be sipped—
though every guide book warns against it—
she took what was offered, she returned the smile.

II.

She has a driver, and this is how he
cautions her: "When you enter the temple
look neither to the right nor to the left. Men
will ask to guide you. You don't need a guide. Here
you can walk alone." And he's right—she needs
no man, though everywhere she looks, to left
or right, here is another eager to lend
a hand: this hand might shelter her beneath
its steady shadow; this hand might lift her
over the awkward step; this hand makes promises
it's soft enough to keep—take this hand, this
hand, this hand. She's not mis-hearing: that's what he's
proposing—have, hold, riches, health. Why not?
Doesn't she like the men of this country?

It's years since she shook off the grip of love's
illusions; and she can grasp a euphemism
when it takes her by the hand. Still, she's stunned:
here's something else, to her dismayed astonishment,
that even she might buy—prospective bride-grooms

right and left, a ring for every finger.
She won't be led, needs no man, no man's hand:
she will not pay. But look: his hands are dancing.
The wrists angle, the fingers curl and fan,
the palms slip through each other's grip, ten crescent moons
at his finger-tips arc through a cloudy sky.
"I have a skill," he says, and he's right, he's right—
before her eyes, plump youth claws into age,
kitten turns pup, boy rises to girl, demon's tail

beats into angel's wing. He has a skill
prized in any world, any world but hers.
She thinks of her country, its icy streets,
the men she left sleeping there, the skill
withering from their frost-gnawed hands; she sees
how they claw their way, dog the shadows, poor
to poorer, sickness into plague; she sees
a bright boy taking up its hand-me-downs,
learning its sneer, its snuffle, its awkward step,
its secret grip. She walks alone, she looks
both ways, she will not pay, but here's a secret:
she likes the men of this country, likes
this man, wishes she could guide him, wishes
it might be right to take that offered hand.

III.

They say she has to barter, and so she barters,
tight-fisted, smirk-mouthed, sly eyed. Disdain:
shop girls shake it out like gilded cloth, avert
embarrassed faces. Disdain: the carvers
curl it off like shavings, sweep away their
polished smiles. Disdain: she winces from herself,
born dupe muddling the right price, weaseling
and worming, slithering through her own slobber
with her shark's tooth, her mongrel's crawl,
her skunk's fine air. Disdain. She slinks from shop to shop

until she enters one that's empty—no
proprietor to be found, the door wide open,
paintings floor to ceiling, the cash box
straining against its rubber band: disdain? or invitation?

Monday, Tuesday, Wednesday—by the time he's
there, she knows his stock as well as he does,
and she knows just what she wants. They say she
has to barter, and so she barters,
wincing from herself, fumbling each clumsy
move. Disdain. To her "how much?" he answers,
"others will cost you less," and shrugs away
the game. Check and mate. She reconsiders.
Where do they go from here? He sits, and she
sits with him, sharing the heat, the sun,
sharing the cool tile floor, sharing the breeze
that sets the paintings knocking in their frames.
She has all day. Wednesday, Thursday, Friday—
they sweat it out. Here's what they find to speak of:

how garlic heals, how rice plumps, how ginger
makes joyful; how rain sluices a leaf and gilds
a lily; how he came to paint, and how she
didn't; how hard it is to draw a hand; how gold
sharpens green; how green shadows gold—she's seen
how it taints; he's seen it feed the hungry,
raise the dead. Friday, Saturday, Sunday—
by the time the sale's agreed, she's profited
like the capitalist she is, she's found
something she didn't know she wanted
like any good consumer. Morning price:
she pays it, holds out her hand to clinch the deal,
and though it's not the custom of this country,
he humors her by holding it between his own.

IV.

The still swan rides the still water, its plumes
a froth of air, its weak feet dangling. Pretty.
Don't be fooled. With no visible activity,
no visible exertion, it comes, comes
into sail, pinions set, a low growl
edging the poised neck's ruffed perfection,
cresting its own wave. White water, white swan,
and on its back a woman like a jewel,
feather firm and feather graceful, rooted
serenely as a feather—why else
ride swan-back? But don't be fooled. With no hint
of agitation, no straining muscle,
no bead of sweat, she's cresting her own wave,
she's burgeoning. Who does she think she is? Oh,

that would be telling. A silent woman
rides a silent swan over silent waters,
in this hand the sprouting rice, the ginger
green for planting; in this hand, the bound leaves
of the *lontar*, rustling its thousand tongues;
in this, the mandolin, its quiver of strings;
in this, the lotus—rooted, flowering—
its open mouth, its eye; here, green silk strung
with gleaming memory; here, passion fruit,
white feathers, a froth of air. Thumb catches finger
in the O of active contemplation—
poised woman, proud swan, unruffled water,
and every arm with its hand out towards you.
Who do you think you are? Open your hand.

My South
in memory of Elize Smith Hodges and Nathalie Heyward FitzSimons

I. Greenwood

It's 1953 and lunch is on the table.
By the steps, liriope wag their sharp tongues,
toss their white, their purple squills; the flat slats
of the porch, swelling with damp heat, begin
imperceptibly to bend; the rockers
tock on their own, the hammock yaws, the glider
faintly squeals. In the dim parlor, a carpet worn thin
lies over the one worn thread-bare, and the four-year-old
lies there too, her palisade of dominoes
turreted with spools, whispering again how Merlin
made the Giants' Reel. The good woman
unties her white apron, smoothes back her grey hair.
She's ready to clear her throat, ready to break the spell.
Lunch is on the table. It is 1953.

It's 1953 and lunch is on the table.
The four-year-old picks her way through black forests
of books in their glass-faced cases, past the piano
that plinks on its own, past the dragon-footed bath
to the dim kitchen, where a thin girl—thin
and brown—stands folding a dish rag. The four-year-old
holds out her hand, and the thin girl follows:
now they can eat, now everyone is there.
The good woman looks at the girl, and the girl
at her mistress, the understanding between them
crackling the air. They know something the child doesn't.
But lunch is on the table: pink rounds of ham,
crab-apples dyed magenta. The child will never
see a servant in that house again.

II. Columbia

It's 1953 and lunch is on the table.
At the road's far end, a susurrus of dust
muffles the mule's steady clop, the cracked voice
crying through the suburbs "Sweet corn. Tomatoes";
while at this end, the fresh-poured tar still spews up
its acrid sweat, the rag-time banjo chatter
of its clinkers, its exodus of ants.
The four-year-old has tarred the yellow sun-dress,
has blacked her hands. Now May will have to scrub
and scrub till she's presentable again.
She eats by herself, she's a big girl, she knows
to clean her plate of every crumb, she knows
what's welcome at the table, knows how white
her hands must be. In the bright kitchen, May

stands munching her tomato like an apple,
lets the juice drip into the sink. Someday
the four-year-old will be this tall. "Know what?"
she says, "I have a monkey," remembering
a dream, the carpet rising with her every breath,
minarets spooling beneath her out-stretched arm.
Now the good woman of this house comes in,
carrying her own cleaned plate. "What's that?" she asks,
and May snorts back, "just another of her lies."
The good woman looks at May, and May looks
at her mistress, the understanding between them
easy as the sun outside. The good woman
takes dinner to May's house every Christmas, every
Easter, every Thanksgiving that May is alive.

III. My South

Say that you're a good woman, and a child
comes to your house. It's a small house, tidy,
just like its neighbors, and you're just like
your neighbors, too: tidy, generous, polite.
No witch lives here. There's no rope, no hood, no knife.
But now you see your house through the child's eyes.
Maybe you've taken one step, or two, to the side
of your neighbors, but we're not talking insight;
maybe you're Christian, but we're not talking wise.
You look at your house, and you think "No child
will learn exclusion at my table," or, "This child
will learn open-heartedness from my honest smile."
The moment comes when you must change your life,
but how will you know when you have changed enough?

I look at the past, and I see what you see.
I too can say "this will not suffice,
this domestic compromise, this domestic lie."
I see the limitation—because they showed me.
So here is your assignment: list out
everything you want that child to learn,
today, tomorrow—all the ways you can
imagine for these women to be good.
You'll have to hurry with your answers.
Already the biscuits are cooling; ham fat
thickens in white ribbons over the string beans;
already melting ice begins to water
the sweetened undercurrents of the tea.
Hurry. Lunch is on the table. It is 1953.

Footwork

1. Map
Ancient Méxica, for Aurora Camacho de Schmidt

How they fled the seven caves; how they tracked
the five winds; how three paths led to the one
water; how the name circled above them
until they called it down—all this is known
by the maps they left, their hesitations
translated to perfect naked footprints,
crescents swollen at ball and bloody heel,
toes precisely numbered, a syncopation
of left and right, as if a man scouted
the damp sand of a lake shore, though there was
no water, no name but cactus spine and
scorpion's sting and rattler, the tribe's slow progress
measured by one man's stride, in retrospect so
resolute, so purposeful, so solitary.

2. Night
Oaxaca, Mexico, for Brian Meunier and Perky Edgerton

The middle of nowhere is like any
where else: people live there, burn their dinners,
stay up late as they dare, hazy sunset
thickening towards shrouded night. Everywhere
air clouds with our breathing; our feeblest light
darkens the sky. So when a traveler
follows his host up the rickety stair
to the roof and sees there—invisible,
even in the middle of nowhere,
from the street below—the stars of childhood
whirling bright as pinwheels at a circus,
as flaming hair, it's worse than a surprise:
it's shame, it's grief at everything, without
perceiving, we've lost sight of, kissed good-bye.

3. Rain
      Ubud, Bali, for Tom Whitman and for Betsy Bolton

"Next time": words for any futurity—
next day, next decade: the indefinite
put on schedule. Rain beats through the thatch, steams
sweat from your back, rips gust and gully down
Monkey Forest Road. "Next time" you sit out
the storm behind the rain's beaded curtain,
opening rambutan, selak, mangosteen.
The lotus ponds spill over, little fish
slip across the stepping stones, and the frogs
speak so deeply that at each step your foot
rings like a bell: *Hati-Hati!* Watch it!
sandals slicked on the rice field's thin mud walls.
This is why you came—dead fan, stopped toilet,
dim lights, swelter: "next time" you feel at home.

4. Bush
      Australia from the air, for Kim Arrow

Beneath us, Eden grows red, grows stippled:
salt bush, blue bush, poverty bush—the trail
of thirst spiraled by dust, by round white stones
among the spinifex, the grey-green wattle.
By eye, by ear, by nose, by hand—a map
worming its way to the tongue: here a man
rocks back on his heels, waiting, thighs angled
like a weapon. Where every foot is known,
only Cain wears shoes, shrouds his steps in blood,
blood and feathers. As a painter journeys
from this edge to that, filling in landscape
as he goes, a man who flies must sing his way
fast as the birds who tune their migrations
to symphonies compressed beneath their tongues.

5. Brink
>   Ulu Watoo, Bali, for Randall Exon

Evil walks straight, but you give it the slip
dodging through the staggered gateway. Bare stone
wrapped in black and white: *lingam* and *yoni*
in holiday best; God lifting his shank, his
white trunk—Ulu Watoo. From the temple's brink
you watch the Indian Ocean churning
aqua and cream at the cliff's foot, thinking
you'll never be farther from home. Meanwhile
the new priest naps, the old priest heats his rice
oblivious. Always the stranger moons
at the ordinary, and not just you:
in Atlanta, the young Thai, delighted—"I
have never seen this"—as the streets empty
of evil and fill with unimagined snow.

6. Tang
>   Botanic Gardens, Sydney, Australia, for Diarmuid Maguire

Quick as that: one step on the sidewalk, the next
on air, flesh evanescing, lungs bursting
with fragrance, frangipani white and waxy
in the city's heart, blushing your breathing
for a block on either side. There's a scent
I first smelled there—a tang like lemon, a
peppery edge—and no one can tell me
what it is: not eucalyptus, not quite
geranium, cooler than that, aloof
but related. Stumbling tantalized past
the dracaena's bladed wedge—dragon tree,
dragon's blood—as if, unexpected and
without knocking, you pass through walls of rose
and lilac into the zest of paradise.

7. Flick
    for Elena Retfalvi

In Lem's novel *Solaris*, the hero
understands that the woman in his bed
is not his wife, but a simulacrum,
not only because his wife is dead, but
also because its feet—dimpled and rosy
as an infant's—have never touched the ground.
Tricks most feet learn so early—to balance
an upright eight times one's length; to buoy
a swaying weight; to take in stride stones, burrs,
throw rugs; to colonize an awkward boot—
it can't manage, crawls instead. Tarkovsky,
filming it, could find no foot so innocent,
screened the cracked heel and callused toe of one
pedestrian, sage, cosmopolitan.

8. Flight
    Alaska, in memory of Michael Durkan

When a heart goes down over the ocean
you take landfall where you can, from tropic
to arctic in a single gasp. Your wings
chatter with frost, skin slicked by the glacier's
tongue, and over the eye a wash of white,
a wash of white, another and another
until the sheer weight shadows blue
and blue silence hangs heavy. Caught between
time zones, half grey-, half day-light, who knows
the hour? Sometimes a gust of white peels off
into nothing. Out there in the wind a man
seals himself in with blocks of ice. His own breath
warms him, and by morning he'll take
heart again, making tracks through fresh snow.

Theseus Drops the Thread

Wakes each night past midnight in a strange bed
to pitch black and vertigo: red sails, white—
which side should he spring from? Shakes out his hands,
throttles the nearest throat. Nails grown long-haired—

someone should shave him, hold his boneless hands
gone soft as if he never sailed: white sails,
black. Like walking through dread, through surf-thick dust,
feet lost in undertow and rip-tide. Don't

get him started. Always the quiet man,
now he jaws and jaws—black sails, red—tongue flared
like a cape, open-mouthed at what comes charging.
Take the bull by its horns, turn cartwheels

through the labyrinths of syntax: he can
still wince, he can still flinch, he can still ache.
Sun etching a shadow, boots scuffing dust,
the white trace of his progress unspooling—

of course he was nonchalant. Red sails, white
sails, black. Wakes past midnight; pees in the sink.
Body never lets on how the dream ends.

Two Little Songs About Love

1. Riding Bottom

Titania's riding Bottom again, her thighs
clamped tight down the whole length of ear, so he'll hear
no airs but the one she's sliding against him,
her skin crazed by the strain, chalk white with the blush
of a bruise just starting. They say he's an ass
for sticking with her, older than midnight and
the moon's own face on, but now she's untangling
his sideburns hair by single black curling hair,
oiling each shaft down the whole of its length so
he's harnessed with light, nuzzling his bristles deep
into the shine of her. Long shanks, long shins, flesh
going soft on the bone, dress up over one
slack hip, straddling him, stroking him, nothing but
herself on offer, and drenched with the offering.

2. Discipline

She's an acrobat balanced on the tip
of her tongue. The very tip. Her very own tongue.
She's worked that muscle. She's sweated it slick.
She'll trust it to extend, flex, hold her up

or back, if need be. She can feel the pinch,
the twisted strands of wire; she can taste blood
as she twirls in place, mouthing the crimson
air. Once she was stiff. Time's made her supple.

Yes, they're acrobats balanced on the tips
of their tongues. The very tip. Each other's tongue.
The merest Freudian slip and they'll plunge
open-mouthed into that long last liquifying

bone-crushing kiss. When she says "he's always on
the tip of my tongue," it's this lapse she intends.

Sweat

The slick palm slips its grip and the world
tips on its axis—loose ball, jump ball, screw ball.
The world's gone woozy, peels off its jacket,
smacks the backboard, thwacks the bat, teeters, spins.
The only breeze we've got is the world's swerving.

One palm slicks another out on the dance floor,
the hip hand slips its juicy grip, silk slithers—
couples careening into the spin, spritzing
the muggy crowd. Open-mouthed, panting
its heart out: blue note, blue moon.

One palm washes the other, brother sears the hand
of brother, the wilting overcoat slips
from the shoulder and off the arm. He's shedding
the winter as if there'll never be another.
Sidewalk grit. Sun-scalded skin.

Damp sheets, dank air, a key riding a kite:
crackle and spit. The river gets goose bumps,
the sky claps its hands, the air opens
in a wet kiss. Rainbows slick the ripples.
The ball nests all night in the pitcher's glove.

A man's sweat wringing out of him as he walks,
a woman pooling before the window fan,
and children incandescent, haloed in thick air.
Wet patches on a dark shirt. Steam clouds the sky
where by night the stars are boiling.

Girls at the Hemingford Grey Regatta
River Great Ouse, July 1996

They've got their hamper stocked with the best provisions,
crustless sandwiches, crisps and colas, magazines;
they've got their parasol propped,
                    tucked through the handle,
held fast by a blue silk scarf; they've got sun-cream
stroked on their shaded faces; they've got the giggles
so fierce they clutch each other. They're maybe thirteen.

They've got eyes for no one rowing on the river—
no proud little lad, no grumbling gran, no mum.
They've got eyes only for Sweet Johnny—darkish, tall-
ish, arms crossed on his thin chest, somewhat underdone
for my taste. He's fifteen, his smooth face undecided
between strong bones or baby-fat, striking or handsome,

clever or genial, leather-black jacket or farm-
blue jeans, James Dean's dark glasses or his own dark eyes.
He's too old for them, too old to notice them,
too young not to notice how he makes them sigh,
not to want to make them sigh some more. Their little note
for him blows in the river. Giggles rock them side to side.

Still, one of them's cool as the Riviera, her face
exquisite, her hair a bright slick of butter.
One day she'll smile on her way to the loo and
tickle her husband's privates so he won't forget her.
How common
            and how rare she is, her friend knows already,
laughter rapid as sun strokes on this dazzling water.

Out

Six months since he walks. Today
he shocks upright, finds his feet,
staggers three steps, four steps, five—

forgets again, collapses. Six months
since he talks: today he laughs outright,
says "Colonel, how de do" and "so they tell me,"

sings, whistles—then he's gone, dead
to the world again, corpse-stiff
on the living room sofa, laid out

flat and fixed, an effigy, only
an eye-lid moving, half up, half down.
Six months eavesdropping on his own dreaming,

thinking whatever it is
he thinks, whatever he can:
Billy Bryan, Jinx and Gin

Gin, Ginievieve; thirty-three, forty
six, eighteen; Nat Lee Caroline Bob
and Charlie: six months, and today he

knows me, I know he knows me,
says "Darlin, don't be such a
stranger." More pills than food, and

he's there again, you can see him, he
can see out, just raising his face, just
clarifying. Grab him, grab his hand

but he's gone back down, the fog
closing over him. Always a drink
on the end table, always

a game on tv—to speak
was to interrupt him, privacy
by means of chaos, sudden exits

in exasperation: where
are you going? Out. Suppose
tomorrow is like today,

suppose he climbs up, remembers how
to rest a foot sole flat on the floor,
brace with the toes, push up from the thigh;

suppose he keeps his balance,
swings his foot loose and forward,
shifts his weight, takes one step and

another, suppose he remembers
all he's forgotten, comes all the way back
to us, will he say where he's been?

V. The Slaking

Two Last Things

1. The Thread

Between him and me was stretched a white thread
knotted tight the morning I was born. Think
of it: that line of white drawing itself
through air, fugitive as a drift of smoke,
curling and curveting, crossing over

and under itself, a bold signature
indelible, flourishing. Think: a thread
between every daughter and father, lines
crossing and uncrossing as the daughter
toddles or the father strays, every year

a cat's cradle complicating and then
gapping open, each family a tangle,
she and he spinning out their gossamer,
riding the wind as far as it takes them,
crossing and re-crossing, binding the world

tight and springy as a baseball. Nothing
so fine, the thread invisible unless
the sun catches it, you could walk through it
and hardly feel its cling. Nothing so strong:
a woman hanging by that single hair.

*****

You see this thread? I'm untying it now,
picking the knot apart, fraying the strands.
Without this ballast, you're going to shimmy
like a skiff pushed out in deep water, you're
going to skitter like a freed balloon,
you'll be the perfect smoke ring puffed out
by an expert, and me, I'll be
trailing this loose end forever.

2. The Harp

My brother's never driven so
deliberately, decelerating
so politely at each light, as
if to say, with gentlemanly

hesitation, "No, after you;
no, you go first." He wants to stop
for doughnuts, wants to show me all
the landmarks, as if I'd never

lived here, hadn't been here only
weeks ago. Says, "Who knows, he might
be with us through the weekend"; says
"Who knows, he might be passing as

we speak."
                He wasn't. At the door
my bags, in the hall my coat, fall
into their sobbing. A chair clears,
and a harp—a harp!—plays "Hark

the Herald Angels." He's become
his own distrusted father, mouth
open, cold. She presses my hand
to his collarbone, hard, perhaps

she means it for his heart. The harp's
insistent, loud, a little sharp.
His toothless mouth. His hair strained back.
He coughs. No reason he shouldn't

cough again, but he never does.
The harpist taught herself. Her harp
found her in Jerusalem. She
never thought she'd be harping out

a friend. Says "He waited for you."
No one believes it. She's brought us
butter mints so succulent they
melt to slow airs on the tongue.

Black Hole

1. Brookgreen Gardens, Say 1957

Brookgreen: such a pretty name for a swamp—
Miss Anna Huntington's half-abandoned
sculpture garden, her aesthete's Eden, her
sanctum by the sea. Shabby years: no brook
that we could find, and not precisely green—
the live oaks sooty and the grasses parched,
the water standing thick and yellowing
in the reflecting pools. Of its former
glory—flood gates, tide fields, the long waters
swaddling the big-grain rice, the thousand
bent and bitter slaves bowed to the yield and
the overseer—Miss Anna, fresh from the North

and, as my Pops said, "eddicated," left
not one shred, except perhaps the Africans
caught in bronze or white marble, mute witness
to the silent politics of art. We
were there in all seasons, five rough children
out from underfoot, a woman harried
beyond her own patience or endurance, learning
the lesson of tension in fixity—
Diana just flexing her bow, a hound
mauling the haunch of Actaeon, Pegasus
rising, Death beckoning, Dawn loosening her
braids of rain, and—unlikeliest of all—

Samson wrestling an alligator,
left hand gripping the snout, right arm strained back
to grapple the tail, staunch *Tau* over upturned
Omega, legs braced taut, and there at the center
a little penis, prize for any child
who could keep quiet about it. Picnics
in the scrub, dust kicked up by our tires
flouring our skin: olive loaf, pickle

loaf, pineapple fished from a can, white bread
soggy with mayonnaise, watermelon
crusted with salt, a chicken-wire fence
unraveling, pinestraw steeping, black logs

rutting, the dangerous deep rippling smile. A painting
I love catches the essence of that marshland:
reeds whispering away from you as far
as the earth can turn, a tawny bristling
crew-cut; bold autumn sky chilling into cirrus,
raising the little hairs on your arms despite
the thick air. This sweep of light so draws the eye
that it's no wonder almost no one sees
at first, in the foreground's rusty muck, that black hole
which is the alligator's eye, just snapping distance
from where you stand, open-mouthed and happy,
wide-eyed, holding out your pointing hand.

2. Zippi-dee-doo-dah

Does misery love company? Ask her
and maybe she'll say, maybe she'll know what
she'd love. All afternoon slumped on the couch
boneless and moping, hair in her eyes and
her mouth sullen, never a word to say
for herself, never lifting a finger—
enough to try a saint's patience. Don't you
want to tidy her, rake back those bangs, mop
that sweaty skin, sit her up straight? All day
the little kids carom about while she
sits oblivious: draggle-tail, ham-fist,
twiddle-thumbs. Send her to the kitchen, she

stares into space, slack-jawed, water splashing
into diamonds in her hands, a fortune
down the drain. Set her to sew, she slouches
squint-eyed over piddling stitches, crumples
the cloth, leaves a snail's slick trail on the skirt

she's hemming. Set her to sweep, she circles,
dawdles, dilly-dallies, tracks her own dirt
back in. Does misery love company?
Sent to her room, she sags, droops, lazes, sighs,
sticks her shiftless nose in a book. Don't
you want to shake some gumption into her,
scrub her mouth out, slap that smirk off her face?

A creature bred to the briars learns fast
to hop to, or else low-crawls through life, fur torn
and skin scabby, sneaky and cringing. That's
what she's made of herself. Grease! Her hair's flat
with it, her face oily, smeared thick with paint—
whited sepulchre, grubby Jezebel,
melancholy seeping into evening
darkening the very air she breathes. Miss
Misery: that peevish pride that flees
her own light. Lazy Bones. Idgit. Good for
you know what. Strident in the dark the
escalating spite: a saint's patience.

Don't you want to scratch her eyes out, snatch her
bald-headed, fry her gizzard? Oh, fling your
sharpest words at her, hurl your hardest hearts—
they'll stick to that impassivity, they'll
tar the mind that sped them. Does misery
love company? Didn't anybody
teach you any better? All night in the briars
the moon stays to herself, the stars sharpen
their claws, the darkness keeps whatever you
throw out there: cotton boll, cotton tail, mean
cotton mouth. So, Daddy Fox and Mama Bear,
what do you say to the baby now?

3. Talk

Bite your tongue if you can't say anything
nice. It's a hard girl who hastens her own
father to his grave, hard to discover
you are that girl—not that he'd say so, your
sweet daddy, poker-faced as ever and
silent as the tomb. Seen but not heard. You want
to talk? she said. So talk. What could you say,
picking apart your snarled and knotted tongue?
Over the blackboard, your fifth-grade teacher
pinned her smug lessons: "superficial people
talk about things; shallow ones talk about
other people; while the superior discuss

ideas"—but what was an idea? And how
might you grow one there behind your gritted teeth,
polish it, spit it out—a little pearl
of disregarded wisdom? She clenches
her fists on the juddering wheel, clenches
her jaw on her fury: talk, she says. She
doesn't mean it, prefers you sullen. Is this
where it started, the close reading, the need to trace
every last nuance in a face or a word?
Someone's put her up to it—not that he'd
say so, your sweet daddy, invisible
as always when you want him, fugitive

as wisdom. A lady never declares
her politics, never mentions money,
never swears to God. Whenever you say
a man's name, she says, we know what to think,
we know what you are. Will they ever forgive you,
those men you named?—anxious Alfred Prufrock,
for all his high talk never quite coming
to the point; pale Ramon Fernandez, cloaked
in quizzical authority, absent
by the sea at Key West; and lost Red Hanrahan,

old lecher with a love on every wind
who'd rather gamble his nights away

than ever stake his heart—forgive your
tarnishing their sterling reputations, blackened
with your own? How you doted on their silence, reading
affection in their impersonal charm, all of them
so like the man who you knew loved you best—not that
he'd say so, tactful to a fault, impartial
as doom. A nice girl never talks about
the toilet, never airs her dirty laundry
for all the world to smell. Is this where it
started, the need to fart, to blurt out the
unspeakable? All that time reading his wince
as sophistication, an irony you thought you shared.

4. Midas' Wife

Midas' wife wakes up listening, wakes up
five, seven, ten, twelve times a night. Sometimes
he's coiled there foetal beside her, and
sometimes he's wandering. She wakes up
listening for that low mutter, for the sh-sh
shuffle of his slippers down the hall. Once
she found him naked on the front porch, once
bruised and fallen in the den. She's learned
how to lift him in a fireman's grip. She's learned
how to wipe his mouth, wipe his nose, wipe
his rear. She's learned how to lead him
by his trembling hand. Midas' wife

wakes up listening, wakes with that jolt
that feels like falling, with the live wire pang
of dread. Sometimes she stretches out a hand
to steady herself and finds him shuddering,
chilling the bed with his shallow sighs. Sometimes
she holds back her breath for minutes at a time,
straining to hear his sluggish heart

over the snort and gallop of her own.
She's waked to weeping, she's waked to silence,
she's waked to find the spread thrown back and him
down and shaking like a dog on the cold floor.
Yes, and sometimes she forgets, reaches out

for the man he was. Midas' wife
wakes up listening for whatever he
might tell her, for the three clear words
in a coughed-out clot of syllables, for
the question that tilts his head, the refusal
that thins his lips and narrows his mulish eye,
the pains that clench his hands, the recognitions
that still spark his fire. She listens so hard,
it's no wonder she speaks for him: "your father,"
she says, "wants you to know" or "wants you
to have." It's surprising how long they
accept that, his children—month after month,

nearly a decade gone, not listening
to what she's not saying, contented
not to hear. And what could she say? Who
could she tell? Who would believe her? Who
would forgive? The king is dead. Long live
the king. "Asses' ears, asses' ears," she
whispers down the telephone's black hole
to the distant one, the absent one, whose tongue
shakes already like her father's, whose ears
fill already with his silence, the one
who understands the need to deny him,
the one who fumbles for a reply.

5. Black Hole

No ideas but in things: two women sit
on a sofa surrounded by, crowded by,
jostled by things, each thing an idea, each idea
interpretable. This half-hemmed child's dress
stitched for a church bazaar, for instance, to one
means piety made palpable, means duty
accepted gladly; for the other, it's
incapacity, it's sloth recognized
so often it feels true, it's the sweet lure
of her own hypocrisy. And this lipstick,
furiously red, dropped among the needles—
for one it's propriety; for the other

a mouth harsh and bitter, a lurid stain.
This portrait of a man, stone-faced and upright,
dead these two hundred years, glows for one
with deserving pride; for the other, blushes
too little with the oppressor's shame. And here,
this album of photographs documenting
each artifact from el Templo Mayor
for one means independence, consciousness,
a passion for the world; to the other
it's self-indulgence, pretentiousness—or
so the younger might believe. No ideas
but in persons: two women sit on a sofa

polite with each other, between them everything
they don't say, haven't said, can't say, won't. It's
imperceptible to the naked eye,
that blotch in the air between them, stubborn
as a smudge from a child's shoe, persistent
as a fruit-fly; it's the shadow scorched deep
when your eyes squinch shut in summer sun; it's
charred galaxies, cinders in the cosmic dark.
No ideas in a black hole: an astronaut
dancing towards that pinprick would find her feet
yanked away from her head, her body thinning,
a thread frayed and bitten, yearning towards the

needle's eye. Stand clear, stand clear, you want to call
to the little ships spiraling ever closer, like
soap suds towards a drain, but there's no need—no fool
would go there, where every word falls hard against
that vast deaf ear, where every memory
is ripped apart, where every thought is broken,
where gravity collapses on itself,
where time comes to an end. These women know
the dangers, know their limits, know
to keep their distance. Never fear: they have no idea,
no intention of risking themselves. Oh, but
think again: think of all that light lost, crushed inside.

On Purchasing a Second Case
of R.W. Knudsen Family Pomegranate Juice

Ah, Persephone, I don't know what to say—
your mother going like that, and not one word
of warning; the air shuddering behind her,
slamming you back; that shocked look on her cold face.
And ever since, you've worn that shock, more faithful
than her mirror; without her, you've turned blunderer,
child hiding out in the old refrigerator,
no air to cry with, chill wicking your shaken
bones, gone cave-blind. I guess it's no wonder
you took those six slick capsules, warming them
against your tongue, shattering their crisp edges
on your back teeth, savoring near-bitterness,
swallowing it down. Not another bite to eat
in all this empty time. I know just how you feel,

I almost said, but in fact I don't. I woke
in the dark, I stretched into it like a cat
waking daily into its own fur. I can't
remember a brighter air, can't call it choking
when it's all I've had to breathe. What's it like,
Persephone, to grow so nested, each root
and twig entwined, the very hairs on your head
knotted up with hers, shadow tangled into light?
I guess it's no wonder you're leaning still
into that phantom embrace. I'd like to tell you
what everyone will tell you—that she persists
in her persistence, that she's searching for you
high and low, that she'll shift every grain of sand,
sift mountains of chaff, even wake the dead

to find you—a woman with a mouth like
a split fruit, driven wailing through the long winter
ravenous for you. I ought to say it

but in fact I won't—not that I don't lie
when I want to. The leaves folding leathery
as they fall, the thick-skinned globes reddening
like a chapped cheek, geodes unexpectedly
packed tight with rubies: imagine cracking one
open, cramming it glittering into a mouth,
lips and tongue stained black as the twilight—
the child who could never get enough. I
cut my tongue on that sharp and bitter doubt.
It started with six seeds in October.
Now they'll blame it all on me—ice storms in winter,

frost in June—all that light broken, that crystal smashed
to fill my emptied glass. A splash of red,
a foaming at the lip—never the jeweled
clarity of wine, never the bright tang
of citrus, but something thicker, clotted,
more opaque: the glistening seeds gnashed; papery
membranes shredded, wadded; the rind pulped dry—
wax in the cup, medicinal, drunk to the dregs.
Eat of this, the prophet promised: it purges
the envious heart. I eat, I drink, I
breathe it in—never enough, Persephone.
Night after night of it, case after case—
so much more I have to swallow
before I try to speak with you again.

The Slaking

There is one story I can hear again
and again, the story where the shoe fits,
where the tempered steel snagged in the cleft rock
eases itself into the proper hand, where
the stranger flings back his hood and Robin
kneels in that verdant heart, where the mourner
complains to the gardener, where the man
with the child on his back stands open-mouthed
half-way across the river as his old name
flows away, where the one who beds the hag
wakes in the morning to the young queen.
Put your hand in my side, he said: yes, yes,
now I see. Not discovery—you knew it
already; not disguise stripped bare; but re-

cognition, the train leaping the synaptic track,
the ship slipping its galactic tether,
the perfect stone skipping its way across
the cloudy nebulae. He promised me
a thing that is not easy: boots of the skin
of a fish. I have worn those boots, I have
worn them down, the leather carp-rosy, the old scales
petaling the sides, a vellum so sheer
my pulse blushed salmon-ruddy through that
suppleness, that tenderness so shocking to the heel.
In those boots I have walked for seven leagues,
I have walked for seven years, the moon
bounding before me, wringing out its white loins
every twenty-eight dreams. In those boots I stood

in the cave where the wheat-sheaf lights the dead
to life, I stood in the ball court and watched
the blood fly, I stood in the cathedral
where even the glass is stained, and I am
no believer. Yes, I have seen the victor run
triumphant into darkness, the vanquished giddy,

drunk with free-flowing rain. Who was that masked man?
And mama, why did he leave us, hi-yo
Silver away? On the fourth day without sleep,
edges began to shimmer, one action
bled into another, the molecules
the atoms veering off into space: what goes
when you choose noon over midnight. As a planet
turns first one cheek and then the other

to best advantage, as a planet
slowly turns its ravaged face to the light,
we come round at last. The moon swells, the moon
empties. Some nights, I swim sleeved in darkness,
a fish flowing into itself, flowering out
of its own elements; some days, I walk the earth
flayed of my skin, and every breeze salts the wound,
my eyes seared, my tongue scalded—coals of fire.
If the skin fits, wear it, fling back the hood, ease your
worn heart from your side, wake in the morning as
the new queen. Re-cognition. This is
what you are, and this is where: so much light spilling
over the lip of the world, it slakes, it dazzles,
it splashes profligate into the trees.

Notes

Spider Bite: This poem refers to two poisonous spiders: the black widow, recognized by the red hour-glass on its stomach, and the brown recluse, which carries a violin-like mark on its back. Rob Mercer, my first cousin, who never to my knowledge was bitten by a spider, died of AIDS.

Fort-Da: The title of this poem is the name Freud gave to a game he perceived that babies play—"Fort - Da," "Here - Gone"—in which the child throws things out of its crib, Freud thought, as a way of learning to manage the mother's absence. Section 3 alludes very tangentially to the story of Orpheus and Eurydice; and perhaps it is necessary now to explain that a bat-wing window was common in automobiles in the 1950s (and later): it was a small triangle set in that angle where the side window meets the front windshield.

Two Sorceries: I'm grateful to the anthropologist Bruce Grant for the premise of the spirit emporium, a contemporary shamanic practice among the Cuna of Panama.

Shirt of Nettles, House of Thorns: The Irish artist Alice Maher is known for her intriguingly twisted imagery—babies' heads cresting in the palms of out-stretched hands, for example, or little Irish step-dancers dwarfed inside their stiff embroidered costumes—and in particular for the objects she constructs from natural materials with the inexorable rightness of folk-lore: a dress made of bees; a tailored shirt made of nettle leaves pieced and pinned together; a small house, about four inches tall, its entire surface studded with thorns.

Floating Gardens: The first of these two myths of origin incorporates phrases from the literature of pre-conquest Mexico:
    —"the circles of jade," "the flowery mist": from a Nahuatl poem describing the *chinampas* of Tenochtitlan, translated by Michael D. Coe from Miguel Leon-Portilla's *Los*

Antiguos Mexicanos a través de sus Cronicas y Cantares, and quoted in Coe's *Mexico From the Olmecs to the Aztecs*, Thames and Hudson, 1994.

—"mountain, water": according to Coe, a Nahuatl double epithet (in which paired nouns imply "a third, inner meaning"), "*atl, tepetl*," signifying "city"; in this system, "*in xochitl, in cuicatl*," "flowers, songs," signifies "poetry."

—"the gods rain down": from the "Song of Xochipilli," Lord of Flowers; quoted in Irene Nicholson's *A Guide to Mexican Poetry Ancient and Modern*, Minutiae Mexicana, 1968, in a chapter excerpted from her *Firefly in the Night: A Study of Ancient Mexican Poetry and Symbolism*, Faber, 1959.

Formic Acid: I gleaned the information about ants contained in this series of poems from various sources, including Michael Chinery's *A Field Guide to the Insects of Britain and Northern Europe*; the *Nova* television presentation, "Ants: Little Creatures Who Run the World"; and (most pervasively) Bert Hölldobler and Edward O. Wilson's *Journey to the Ants: A Story of Scientific Exploration*. I found especially evocative their description of the rare Leptanilline colony (not quite so rare as I imply), which in their phrase "shimmered like a rippling membrane on the surface of the wood when first exposed"; and the description of Amazon ants they quote from William Morton Wheeler's 1910 treatise, *Ants: Their Structure, Development, and Behavior*. "While in the home nest they sit about in stolid idleness or pass the long hours begging the slaves for food or cleaning themselves and burnishing their ruddy armor, but when outside the nest they display a dazzling courage and capacity for concerted action." Nor is this martial imagery out of place: according to Hölldobler and Wilson, "If ants had nuclear weapons, they would probably end the world in a week."

Black Hole: Brookgreen Gardens is a sculpture park, located just north of Charleston, South Carolina, founded in the 1930s by the American representational sculptor Anna Hyatt Huntington and her husband, the philanthropist Archer Milton Huntington. The statues mentioned in the poem can all be found there. The painting I refer to in the last stanza is by Philadelphia artist Sarah McEneany. "Zippi-dee-doo-dah" is the title of a song from Walt Disney's cinematic version of the Uncle Remus stories, *Song of the South*. The men mentioned in "Talk" are, of course, figures from the work of T.S. Eliot, Wallace Stevens, and William Butler Yeats. "Old lecher with a love on every wind" is a line from Yeats' poem "The Tower." For Midas' ears, see Ovid's *Metamorphoses*, xi, 146 ff. "No ideas but in things" is quoted from William Carlos Williams' *Paterson*. For information about astronomical black holes, I referred to Stephen W. Hawking's *A Brief History of Time*. The phrase "cinders in the cosmic dark" was suggested by a PBS special on black holes.

The Robert McGovern Publication Prize is awarded to poets over 40 who have published no more than one book. The prize is established in memory of Robert McGovern, poet, professor, co-founder of the Ashland Poetry Press, and long-time chair of the English Department at Ashland University. Manuscripts are submitted by nomination only. The McGovern nominating panel currently consists of Alice Fulton, Andrew Hudgins, Philip Levine, Robert Phillips, Eamon Grennan, William Heyen, John Kinsella, Annie Finch, Carolyn Forché, Vern Rutsala, Richard Jackson, Gregory Wolfe and Gerry LaFemina. The co-winners of the 2005 McGovern Prize are as follows:

Maria Terrone, for *A Secret Room in Fall* (nominated by Gerry LaFemina)
Nathalie F. Anderson, for *Crawlers* (nominated by Eamon Grennan)

Former winners of the McGovern Prize:

A.V. Christie, for *The Housing* (nominated by Eamon Grennan)
Jerry Harp, for *Gatherings* (nominated by John Kinsella)